Grandmother's Memories

A Keepsake Journal

Journal Ideas For Everyone

I'd love to know more about you
when you were younger

Your Photo Here

What were you like as a child?

What were your favorite childhood memories?

Who were your childhood friends?

Where did you meet your childhood friends?

Where was your neighborhood? How was it like?

What household chores did you do when you were a child?

What were your hobbies? Do you still do them today?

What was your favorite sport?

What was your favorite subject in school? How about the least favorite?

What was your most favorite time of the year? Is it still your favorite now?

Your Photo Here

What was your first job? Did you love it?

Recipe: Serves:

Recipe: *Serves:*

Did you ever need stitches? Did you have broken bones?

Did you have a childhood crush? Who was it?

Who were your favorite celebrities back in the day?

What was famous back then? Are they still famous now?

Which household chores did you dislike the most? Which were your favorite?

What did your friends call you back in school? How did you feel about it?

What were your favorite subjects? Which did you like least?

Where was your favorite hangout place? Who did you go with?

What did you learn as a child that you would like to teach me?

What did you enjoy doing on weekends?

What did you enjoy doing in Spring? Summer? Fall? Winter?

What were your favorite movies? TV shows?

Now I'd love to know more
about how you felt when you
found out me

How did you feel when you found out you were going to be a grandma?

Our first photo together

What were some stuff you bought for me before I was born?

Describe how you felt when you held me for the first time.
Include where, when, and what happened.

What things did you purchase in the first weeks I was born?

MORE PHOTOS OF YOU AND I!

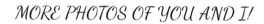

Describe how you felt when you started seeing me crawl. Walk. Run.

Did you have to child-proof your house because of me? What did you do?

MORE PHOTOS OF YOU AND I!

What were my first words to you? How did you feel?

Where did you like taking me when I was still a baby?

What activities did you do with me when I was a baby?

MORE PHOTOS OF YOU AND I!

Describe my 1st birthday celebration. What did you wear? What did you give me?

What stories did you like telling me?

Describe our first Christmas together. Did you cook?

Describe our first Thanksgiving together. Did you cook?

What was your favorite trip with me? Describe it.

MORE PHOTOS OF YOU AND I!

What are your wishes for me as I grow older?

Which places would you like you and I to visit?

Write a letter to me as you watch me grow. Let me know how you feel, what you'd like me to know, etc.

What are words of wisdom that you'd like to share with me?

MORE PHOTOS OF YOU AND I!

Made in the USA
Monee, IL
16 December 2021

85906158R00033